春潮 NOV+

今 晚 ……
要 么 早 点 睡

汉 英 对 照

LOVE POEMS

{ for married people }

[美] 约翰·肯尼（John Kenney）/ 著　武玉江 / 译

中信出版集团 | 北京

图书在版编目（CIP）数据

今晚……要么早点睡：汉英对照 / (美) 约翰·肯尼著；武玉江译. -- 北京：中信出版社，2020.10

书名原文：Love Poems for Married People

ISBN 978-7-5217-1999-4

Ⅰ.①今… Ⅱ.①约…②武… Ⅲ.①英语—汉语—对照读物②诗集—美国—现代 Ⅳ.①H319.4：Ⅰ

中国版本图书馆CIP数据核字(2020)第112738号

今晚……要么早点睡（汉英对照）

著　　者：［美］约翰·肯尼
译　　者：武玉江
出版发行：中信出版集团股份有限公司
　　　　　（北京市朝阳区惠新东街甲4号富盛大厦2座　邮编　100029）
承　印　者：北京通州皇家印刷厂

开　　本：787mm×1092mm　1/32　　印　张：5.25　　字　数：20千字
版　　次：2020年10月第1版　　　　印　次：2020年10月第1次印刷
京权图字：01-2020-4283
书　　号：ISBN 978-7-5217-1999-4
定　　价：39.80元

献 给 ~~芭 芭 拉~~

~~卡 伦~~

~~帕 姆~~

~~法 国 小 姐~~

~~克 劳 汀~~

~~蕾 蒙~~

丽 莎

For ~~Barbara~~

~~Karen~~

~~Pam~~

~~Miss France~~

~~Claudine~~

~~Ramone~~

Lissa

所有的诗人都写烂诗。

All poets write bad poetry.

糟糕的诗人出版它们，优秀的诗人焚烧它们。

——翁贝托·埃科

Bad poets publish them, good poets burn them.

— Umberto Eco

我尊重你和爱情，
但我和同事在酒吧里忘却了时间

在法国，傍晚五点到七点的茶歇聚会曾是神圣不可侵的，
是约会，亦是男女之事的
委婉说法。

但我们不在法国。
我们在这儿，新泽西，蒙特克莱尔。
时间已过七点，
而我保证过六点到家。

现在的我，满嘴酒气。
下班后与几个同事出去喝了一杯……
好吧，三杯。

我确实忘了买牛奶，
忘了买面包、意大利面，还有过敏药，
也没做引体向上。

你怎么穿得这么正式？
等等，今天是情人节？

I honor you and our love but I also lost track of time at a bar with my coworkers

In France, *cinq à sept* was once sacrosanct,
a euphemism for rendezvous,
for the thing that men and women do.

But we are not in France.
We are here, in Montclair, New Jersey.
And it is well past seven.
And I promised to be home at six.

And, yes, that's booze on my breath.
The guys and I had one . . . fine, three drinks after
    work.

And apparently I have forgotten the milk.
And the bread and the pasta and the pull-ups.
And the allergy medicine.

Why are you dressed up?
Wait. Today is Valentine's Day?

今晚有性趣吗

有啊。
哄睡孩子，
吃点简餐，
沐浴，
或许小酌一杯。
然后，
做那件只想和你做的事——
躺在床上，刷着手机。

Are you in the mood?

I am.

Let's put the kids down.

Have a light dinner.

Shower.

Maybe not drink so much.

And do that thing I would rather do with you than
    anyone else.

Lie in bed and look at our iPhones.

我们的爱情

我们的爱情如同巴黎艺术桥上的挂锁，
成百上千把锁，象征坚不可摧的爱情。
很美好，不是吗？

繁多的挂锁，对于桥梁，已然过于沉重。
你没听说？
反正我在哪儿读过。

桥梁的负重不断增加，
解决方案
是用钳子剪下挂锁，
扔进垃圾桶。
也很美好，不是吗？

至此，人们不再被彼此紧锁，
可以自由地注目他人。
这很有趣。

Our love

Our love is like the padlocks on the Pont des Arts, in Paris.
Thousands of locks, symbols of unbreakable love.
Isn't that beautiful?

Apparently, though, all those locks are
too heavy for the bridge.
Did you hear this?
I read it somewhere.

The locks are weighing the bridge down.
So you know what they're going to do?
They're taking them off with bolt cutters and throwing
    them in the trash.
Isn't that beautiful, too?

So now the people aren't locked together anymore.
They're free to maybe see other people.
I thought that was interesting.

你为什么要跟我一起洗澡

莫非浴缸缩水了？

我问。

我们正一起洗澡，

赤裸着，

如同我们从前一直会做的那样。

还记得吗？当初，

我们淋浴、聊天，彼此轻柔地避让，

友善诙谐地共享花洒的水流。

可如今，

你在这儿干吗呢？

我都冻着啦！

洗发水进我眼了！

你刚踩我脚了！

拜托，哪位在冲马桶？

我这儿只剩热水，烫得够泡茶了！

给我出去！

马上！

宝贝，其实这个点子不错，

不过，劳驾能把门带上吗？

Why are you in the shower with me?

Did the bathtub shrink?

I ask because here we are,

naked,

showering together,

like we once did all the time.

Remember? At the beginning?

We would stand and talk,

seals slipping by one another,

a playful ease letting the other into the stream.

Now?

I'm not sure what you're doing in here.

I'm freezing.

There's shampoo stinging my eyes.

You just stepped on my foot.

For the love of Christ who flushed the toilet?

Because I'm being scalded alive.

Get out. Now.

It was a nice idea though, honey.

Could you close the door?

你莫非在撩我

孩子们终于入睡，
而你，正如此这般地
看着我，
挑逗。

又或者
你只是在放空？
等等，
没错，
你只是在放空。

你拉下裙子的拉链，
松垮的内裤
在腰上提得老高。
它们，贵庚几何？

你套上些运动裤，
还有 T 恤、毛衣和抓绒外套，
我已无法辨认

你身体的曲线。

你向我抛送信号的手法，
和那些已婚夫妇间所用的
如出一辙。

正因如此，我们都很清楚，
你想表达：
我要给我姐打个电话，然后点份寿司。
你也干点儿啥吧。

Is it possible you are sending me a sexy signal?

The kids are finally down
and you are looking
at me in that way.
Tease.

Or are you
just spacing out?
Wait.
Yup,
you're spacing out.

You unzip your skirt
and your baggy underpants
ride way, way up on your hips.
How old are those, anyway?

You pull on some sweatpants
and a T-shirt and a sweater and a fleece
and I am not able to

make out any contour of your body at all.

I think you are sending me
a signal in the way that
married couples
send each other signals.

And just so we're clear
you're signaling
I'm going to call my sister and order sushi.
You should do something, too.

你是独特的

我想与你分享我的生活。

我这样做了。

当着所有亲朋好友，

包括在你那令人厌烦的家人面前，

承诺过。

你是独特的，

这是我们相遇时

我得到的感受。

我告诉朋友：

他是独特的。

（他们说你没啥特别的。）

现在，我们已结为一生一世的夫妻，

对吗？

（哇，这好像已经是很久远的事了！）

但我想告诉你，

我们相遇后，你确实不一样了。

在某知名婚恋网的用户简介里，你自称：

我喜欢跑步、徒步和烹饪！

你做过一顿饭吗？

你跑步的爱好早被按了暂停键。

我想过无数次，你那

胡扯的简介，

若能重写，

设想下，

我们该如何描述你？

我喜欢坐着，

不洗澡，

爱把手放在短裤前，挠自己的蛋蛋，

时不时抬头看眼刚娶的媳妇，

来句："怎么了？"

对你的妻子而言，这是句多么怪异的问候。

You are different

I want to share my life with you.

I do.

I said those words

in front of all our friends.

As well as your incredibly annoying family.

You're different.

That's what I thought

when we met.

I told my friends.

He's different.

(They said you weren't.)

And now we are married

for life.

Is that right?

(Wow! That seems really long now!)

But here's something.

You're different

from, like, when we met.

Your OkCupid profile said

I like running and hiking and cooking!

Have you ever cooked?

And you seem to have parked that running thing for
a while.

I'm kind of thinking a lot of that was

bullshit.

If we were to redo your profile

hypothetically

what would we write?

I like sitting.

Not showering.

*I enjoy putting my hand down the front of my shorts and
scratching my balls.*

And occasionally looking up at my new wife

and saying what's up.

Which is a weird thing to say to your wife.

酸奶

你带着孩子们
去了乔氏超市，
好让我打个工作电话。

你采购了一周的吃穿用品，
而我的电话改了时间，
于是我刷了会儿视频。

三小时转瞬即逝，
也许我中间睡了会儿？

我会如实交代我没做的事。
我没按你的嘱咐
清空洗碗机。

没洗衣服，
没联系水管工，
也没做另一件你嘱咐过但我忘了的事。

现在，看你忙里忙外，
寻思着你一天的付出，
我想真挚地道声谢谢。

不过，疑惑掩盖了感激之情。
听上去可能很不客气，
看着你的表情，我也知道自己很浑蛋，
但坦白讲，你怎么能忘了买酸奶呢？

Yogurt

You went to Trader Joe's.
And took the kids.
So I could do a work call.

You bought the week's shopping.
And my call was canceled.
So I scrolled around YouTube.

I don't really know where the three hours went.
Though maybe I napped?

I'll tell you what I didn't do.
I didn't unload the dishwasher
like you asked.

Or switch the laundry.
Or call the plumber.
Or that other thing you asked that I forgot.

And now, watching you put away the groceries
surveying all you've done for us today
I feel the need to thank you.

Well, more a question than a thanks.
And granted the tone of it isn't great.
And from your expression I know now I'm fucked.
But seriously, how did you forget the yogurt?

你打算何时关上你的电子书

他们说，爱是光芒。

我觉得他们说过，

但不太确定，

也许是在斯巴鲁汽车广告里听过。

关键是，此刻我在你身上看到了光芒。

我希望没看到，

因为我真的很疲惫。

我刚度过了漫长的一天，

明天还需早起，

而所有这些，你都知道。

他们还说，一个人能知晓一件事，但也会马上遗忘，

如同一条记忆短暂的金鱼。

当我烦躁时，我不住地叹息，

但你充耳不闻，

因为你戴着耳机，

欣赏着一个在布丁上人体冲浪的视频，

而我还以为你在读书。

也许爱就是光芒，
因为它可以变暗、褪色、完全熄灭。
讲真，你到洗手间去看，会死吗？

When are you planning to turn off your Kindle?

They say love is light.

I think they do.

I'm not really sure.

I might have heard that in a Subaru commercial.

The point is that I see your light right now.

And I wish I didn't.

Because I'm really tired.

And I had a long day.

And I have to get up early tomorrow.

All of which you know.

Another thing they say is that a man can know a thing
but forget it almost instantly.

Like a goldfish.

I sigh the sigh I sigh when I'm annoyed.

But you don't hear me.

Because you have earbuds in.

And are watching what appears to be a video of people
body-surfing on pudding.

And here I thought you were reading a book.

Maybe love is like light.
In that it can dim, fade, go out completely.
Seriously. Would it kill you to watch that in the
    bathroom?

约会之夜

你在给谁……

什么?

……发信息呢? 我只想……

抱歉, 什么事?

你正在发信息, 我只是……

是客户。抱歉, 稍等, 他们想改个……

什么?

会议。现在改成明天了。

哦, OK, 好吧。我想看看……

搞定。你在给谁……

一秒钟, 抱歉, 该死。

工作?

什么?

你的工作吗?

稍等, 我告诉过他们文件在哪儿的。

谁?

什么?

没事。

搞什么啊? 在那个 U 盘里, 他们知道的啊……

你说什么？

什么？

没什么。

这家餐厅还不错。

什么？

Date night

Who are you . . .

What?

. . . texting. I was just wondering . . .

Sorry. What?

You're texting and I just . . .

Client. Sorry. Wait. They're changing a . . .

What?

Meeting. Tomorrow now.

Oh. Okay. Well. I guess I'll check . . .

Done. So. Who are you . . .

One second. Sorry. Fuck.

Work?

What?

Is it work?

Wait. I told them where the file was.

Who?

What?

Nothing.

Dammit. It's on the thumb drive. They know that . . .

What is?

What?

Nothing.

This restaurant is nice.

What?

就寝时间

此刻我们在卧室里，穿着内衣。

把灯光调暗些。

不，再暗些。

嗯，用专业术语，应该是关闭电源。

要不塞条毛巾，

挡住门下漏光的缝隙？

不要抱抱吗？

我是指，没有实质性接触的拥抱。

我们都躺在

属于自己那半边床的

边缘。

为什么感觉像张单人床？

你靠得太近了。

提个情趣小建议：

我们闭上双眼，

看谁能保持最长时间，

接下来，试着闭上七个小时。

我喜欢你。

Bedtime

Now we are in the bedroom in our underpants.

Let's turn the lights down.

No, further.

Off, I guess, is the technical term.

Maybe try a towel under the door

where that sliver of light is coming in.

What if we cuddle?

And by cuddle I mean not actually touch.

Each of us at the far edge

of our own side

of the bed.

Why does this feel like a twin bed?

You're so close.

I have a fun sexy idea.

Let's close our eyes

and see who can keep them closed the longest.

For the next, like, seven hours or so.

I like you.

我吸着你的口气

在梦境中，
但我的感觉如此真实。

一个男人，是你吗？
差远了。

是罗博，凯西的丈夫，
带着意大利口音。

我们在海滩上，
是罗博和我，不是你。

他调皮地
追着我，我们笑着。

接着，我的上衣滑落，
"糟糕"，我咯咯地笑着，
他随即抓住我。

然后，一股呛鼻的气息，
犹如烂菜叶、腋臭、死亡。

我眨着眼睛，清醒过来，
你呼出的气息灼热我的面庞。

你这个臭家伙。
罗博，快回来。

I breathe you

I am dreaming
but it feels so real.

A man. Is it you?
Not even close.

It's Rob, Casey's husband.
The one with the Italian accent.

We are on a beach.
Rob and me, not you.

He chases me
playfully. And we laugh.

Then my tops falls off.
Oops, I giggle.
And he catches me.

And then, a terrible smell.
Like garbage. Wet dog. Death.

I am blinking and awake
your breath hot on my face.

You son of a bitch.
Rob, come back.

纵欲

秋，
凉爽多云，
院子里飘荡着
木材燃烧的味道。

我们决定
去高大的树篱下
耙些树叶。

你哆哆地说，
我们没垃圾袋了。
在你耸肩的瞬间，我隐约看见
乳房的跳动。

若它们没被罩在
羊毛套头衫
与工装衬衫下。

好吧，我要回屋了，

你过了一会儿说道。

之后，我们热了点儿牛肉罐头，

随后你上床休息，

我看了半部马特·达蒙的《谍影重重》。

我提到"纵欲"了吗？

抱歉，我或许有些迷糊了。

我想说，咱们"终于"打扫院子了。

Orgy

Autumn
overcast and cool
woodsmoke-scented air
leaves in the yard.

We decided to go out back
among the tall hedgerows to
rake and bag the leaves.

You said in a very sexy voice
We're out of garbage bags.
And in your shrugging I might have seen
your breasts move

had they not been covered under
your fleece
sweatshirt
and work shirt.

Well. I'm going in, you said after a while.
Later, we heated up Dinty Moore beef stew
and then you went to bed.
I watched half of a Jason Bourne movie.

Did I say orgy?
Sorry, my mind wandered.
I meant yard work.

浴室的门

微不足道的小事，
没什么大不了的，
但我想我错过了
家庭会议上的
共同决议。
这是个好提议：
当你在小便时
可以保持浴室门
敞开，
我路过时
你可以微笑着挥手，
说句"嗨，宝贝！"
然后随便和我聊两句。
看看
都发生了些什么——
我心中的爱凋零了些许，
我的身体也凋零了些许。

Bathroom door

Super minor point.
Not a big deal at all.
But I think I missed
the family meeting
where we decided
it was a good idea
to keep the bathroom door
open
while you are urinating
smiling and waving
saying *hey hon*
and trying to talk to me
when I pass by.
See
what happens to me
is that the magic dies a little.
I die a little.

在厨房的洗碗池边

我对你
充满了
欢喜。

当你在洗碗池边
为我做着
肩部按摩。

多么贴心的
小惊喜。

随后，你
托起我的胸
发出"嗯嗯"的声响。

瞬间，
我感到恶心、
悲伤和遗憾。

At the kitchen sink

I was feeling
fondness
for you

As you gave me
a shoulder massage
at the sink.

What a small
lovely surprise.

And then you
cupped my boobs
and made a *wha-wha* noise.

And in an instant
I felt disgust
and sadness and regret.

备孕历程

若在我十六岁时，

你告诉我，

一个美丽的女子

会要求每天和我做爱，

我肯定会说，这不可能。

而现在

下班后飞奔离开，

准点到家。

排卵日，

浓情蜜意的床笫之欢，

但这和高档健身房的预约私教课也没啥两样。

你满怀柔情地对我低语：

"希望你这几天没打飞机，

因为医生说你需要攒够精子数量。"

哦，

好吧，

嗯，关于这事我有个坏消息。

The fertility process

If you had told me

when I was sixteen

that a beautiful woman would demand sex from me

 every day

I would have said impossible.

But here we are

having rushed home from work.

On the clock.

Egg dropped.

Sweet, sweet lovemaking.

But also not unlike a class at Equinox that you have

 to pre-sign up for.

You whisper sweet nothings to me.

I really hope you haven't been masturbating

because the doctor said you need to build up sperm.

Oh.

Okay.

Well, I have some bad news on that front.

再加点料

这，就是我们
在墨西哥餐厅里点餐时
你说的话。
我说：
哎哟妈呀，
你不是在开玩笑吧？
你笑着说：
完全没有啦，
调料好棒棒哦！
你用奇怪的语气说完，
就大笑起来，
好似是对那怪异语气的自嘲。
接着我说：
最好是加个女的，
别是男的。
你问：
你在说什么呢？
我说：
你不是在聊

性爱吗?
你脸上的神情数次转换后,
重归先前的模样。
你说:
我说的是混酱,或许也可以
再来点儿墨西哥沙拉。
我说:
哦,
好的,
这个想法也挺不错的。

Let's spice things up

That's what you said

when we were ordering

in the Mexican restaurant.

And I said

Ohmigod

are you serious?

And you smiled

and said *totally.*

Spicey is nicey you said

in a weird accent

laughing

but also a little embarrassed at the weird accent

    thing.

And I said

it would have to be with a woman though

not a guy.

And you said

What are you talking about?

And I said

aren't you talking about

having a threesome?

You get a look on your face sometimes.

And you got it here.

And you said

I was talking about getting the mole and maybe some

    pico de gallo.

To which I said

Oh.

Okay.

That's a good idea, too.

你们离开时，我哭了

独自一人
矗立在人行道，
汽车驶离时
我挥着手。
你，孩子们，狗。

再见！我说，
再见，大家！

到北部你妈那儿过个长周末，
多惬意的事，
但老爸我有工作要做。

还好，工作量不是很大，
顶多就几小时，
而且说实话，截止日期在两周后。
我当然也能与你们同去。
真该死。

但现在你们已经出发。

回到屋内，

孑然一身，

四下环顾，

宁静祥和，

穿着裤衩，

几箱啤酒，

这就是你们离开时，

我为何热泪盈眶。

I cry as you drive away

Standing on the sidewalk
alone
I wave
as the car pulls away.
You, the kids, the dog.

Bye! I say.
Bye, guys!

A long weekend at your mother's upstate.
What fun.
But Dad has work to do.

Well, not a lot of work.
It shouldn't take more than a few hours actually.
And truth be told it's not due for two weeks.
I certainly could have gone.
Shoot.

But now you've driven away.

And I am here.

Alone.

At home.

In the quiet.

Without pants.

And there's so much beer.

That's why I'm crying

as you drive away.

现在这么做合适吗

站在玄关，

等待出发，

脚拍打着地面。

（我们要去参加我姐的生日聚会，已经晚了。）

转身看到你，

站立在厨房，

仿佛一个男人，在夏日午后的湖边

随意摆弄着手中的鱼竿，

不过那不是一根鱼竿，

而是一把指甲刀。

你正剪着指甲，

在洗碗池边。

你抬起头，或许是看到了我的表情，

你说，怎么了？

如果你还不明白，

我也无力再多解释。

Is this the right time for that?

Standing at the door
ready to go
tapping my foot.
(We are late to my sister's surprise party)
I turn and see you
standing in the kitchen
like a man on a summer afternoon by a lake
casually adjusting a fishing pole.
Only it's not a fishing pole.
It's fingernail clippers.
And you are cutting your fingernails
over the sink.
You look up and perhaps because of the expression
    on my face
you say, *what?*
It would be impossible for me to explain
if you don't already understand.

灯芯绒

就在这几天，
你用指责的口吻
对我说：
嗯，我想我连条灯芯绒裤子都没了。

一、我没扔过你的裤子。
二、我从没见你穿过灯芯绒。
三、现在是六月。

Corduroys

Just the other day
you said to me
accusatorily
Well, I guess I don't have any corduroys *anymore.*

One, I did not throw out your pants.
Two, I have never seen you wear corduroys.
Three, it's June.

很显然，用手机玩暧昧不是这样的

我无从知晓
在进行这种每月定时定量
如同广播体操般的性生活时，
若我向大学室友玛丽发条短信，
你是否会感到失落。

她回：是否看过《王冠》？
我回：看过 !!! 神剧啊。
    我超爱
    克莱尔·芙伊。

我想我被你的表情吓到了，
显然你很错愕：
我竟在用手机
和别人玩暧昧。

但你说，
这不是在
玩暧昧。

于是我发信息问玛丽这是不是，她回：
哈哈哈!!! 你不会真的正在啪啪啪吧？

我说刚才是，但现已停工。
你冲出房间，
绊了下，
跌倒在客厅。

玛丽说：
这有点儿搞笑。
我回了个笑脸表情，
因为，这确实有点儿搞笑。

Sexting isn't this, apparently

I did not know
during the monthly rote calisthenics of our sex
that you would be upset
if I sent a quick text message to my college
    roommate Marie

    who texted back and asked if I'd watched
    The Crown.
    I texted *yes!!! It's amazing.*
    I love
    Claire Foy.

And I guess I was surprised
and from the look on your face
you were certainly surprised
that I was sexting.

    Except you said
    that's not sexting.

So I texted Marie to ask her and she texted back
LOL!!! Are you really having sex right now?

I said I was but not anymore.
You had stormed out of the room and
tripped and
fell in the hall.

And Marie said
That's a little funny.
I sent a smiley emoji
because it was a little funny.

艾米丽的名字不是瑞秋

你记得很多没用的东西，

"二战"中的战役名，

制宪会议的相关史实，

2004 年后的波士顿红袜队先发阵容，

电影《虎豹小霸王》里的对白，

但在去参加邻居家聚会的路上，

你问了个你已问过无数遍的问题，

有一百遍，或者一千遍？

加里的妻子叫什么？是瑞秋吗？

不，不是瑞秋，她从不叫瑞秋，是艾米丽。

她是波士顿人吧，你说。

不，什么呀？当然不是，她是洛杉矶人。

哦，那谁是波士顿人？她的前夫格雷格？

她没有前夫，也没人叫格雷格。是加里，只有……加里。

我以为瑞秋在波士顿那边结过婚。

你在说什么？

他们的孩子叫彼得和格蕾丝，对吗？

你太离谱了，他们叫阿斯特丽德和科莱特。

奇怪，我发誓……

你知道地址吗？我问。

当然，梧桐巷 248 号。

金莺街 9 号，我说。

真的吗？我到底在想谁呢？

不知道，但拜托，告诉我你没忘带啤酒和葡萄酒。

……那当然。

Emily's name isn't Rachel

You remember so much that isn't useful.
World War II battles and
facts about the Constitutional Congress.
The Red Sox lineup from 2004 and
dialogue from the movie *Butch Cassidy and
   the Sundance Kid.*
But on the way to the neighbor's party
you ask the question you always ask.
The one you've asked a hundred times. A thousand?
What's Gary's wife's name? Is it Rachel?
Nope. It's not Rachel. It's never been Rachel. It's
   Emily.
And she's from Boston, you say.
No. What? No. She's from Los Angeles.
Huh. Who's from Boston? Her ex-husband Greg?
No ex-husband. No one named Greg. Gary. Just . . .
   Gary.
I thought Rachel had family in the Boston area.
What are you talking about?

And their kids are Peter and Grace, right?

Not even close. Astrid and Colette.

Weird. I could have sworn . . .

You have the address? I ask.

Oh sure. 248 Sycamore Lane.

9 Oriole Street, I say.

Really? Who the heck am I thinking of then?

No idea. Just please tell me you remembered the
    beer and wine.

. . . Absolutely.

醒来后才意识到，
我在你的生日聚会上调戏了你的闺密

头疼得厉害，
还好我身上从头到脚
都还套着衣服。
我想我该先道歉，
但我很想先喝杯咖啡。
宝贝？
哎呀？
为什么我的衣服会在屋外草坪上？

On waking late and realizing that I hit on your best friend at your birthday party

My head hurts
and I am still fully clothed.
I guess sorry is in order.
But I would kill for a coffee first.
Honey?
Hello?
Why are my clothes on the lawn?

亲密关系心理咨询（第一部分）

亲密关系咨询师
建议我们
重复对方
刚说过的话。

"好的。我听到你说，
我是一个糟糕的丈夫、
糟糕的男人和糟糕的人。"

"等等，罗杰，"咨询师说，
"那不是艾米说的。"
"是的，但我听到的就是这个意思。"
"好吧，但她实际上说的是，她希望你能多倾听一些。
让我们试着重复对方真正所说的话，
而不是自己的诠释。"

抱歉，我刚才没在听……

但我没有说出内心的独白。

不幸的是，我说：

"你这里有 Wi-Fi 吗?"

Couples counseling (part 1)

The couples therapist urges
us to repeat
what each of us
has just said.

Okay. So I hear you saying
that I am a terrible husband,
man, and human being.

Hold on, Roger, the therapist says.
That's not what Amy said.
Yes, but that's what I heard.
*Okay but what she actually said was she wanted you to
    listen more.*
Let's try to repeat the actual words
and not our interpretation.

Sorry, I wasn't listening . . .

But I don't say that part out loud.

Unfortunately, what I do say is,

Do you have Wi-Fi here?

你在想谁呢

你，

当然是你，

我还会在想谁呢？

我的同事阿莱克斯，总是一身古铜色肌肤的那位？

或是健身房的那位卡洛斯？

拜托。

我们的爱情比这更深，克雷格，

我是说戴瑞，

我知道你的名字是戴瑞，

但不知怎么，我想到了星巴克的克雷格，

蓝眼睛的那位，

但你是我的丈夫，我们已定下誓言一生相守。

是的，在这些亲密的时刻，我想起了你。

我的意思是，你当然会划过我的脑海。

你在那儿，

和其他人一起。

如果这是部电影的话，你会出现在演职员名单中，

虽然排名靠后。

"穿毛衣的男子"。

只是……嘘——好了，

不用担心。

Who were you thinking about?

You.

Of course you.

Who else would I have been thinking about?

My coworker Alex, who always seems tan?

Or Carlos from SoulCycle?

Please.

Our love is deeper than that, Craig.

I mean Daryl.

I know your name is Daryl.

But right then I was thinking of Craig from Star-
    bucks who has those blue eyes.

But you are my husband and we are married for life.

And yes I think of you
    during these intimate moments.

By that I mean you certainly cross my mind.

You're in there.

In the mix.

You would be in the credits if it were a movie.

Way down though.

Guy in sweater.

Just . . . shhh.

Don't worry about it.

我们该几点去机场

我订的车七点来。

但起飞时间不是九点半吗？

是啊，怎么了？

七点，哦，好吧，你不觉得七点出发太赶了吗？

九点半的航班，还好吧。

好吧，随你，你想怎么样就怎么样吧。

别这样，要不改成六点四十五？

好啊。

真的吗？太早了吧？

如果是我的话，我会六点十五出发，或者六点。

405 号高速路是个噩梦。

但我们已办好了登机手续，而且没有行李托运。

啊？你怎么搞的？难道忘了安检的长队吗？

你怎么这么说话？

那随你便吧。

我现在打电话，改成六点。

五点四十五可能更明智些。

你在开玩笑吧？

我不准备拿堵车开玩笑。

你又不是没坐过车。

听着，我只想说如果是我的话，我会订在五点半，五点半出发。

为什么不五点出发？

我不知道这是不是你的讽刺，但我百分百同意。

好吧，那我现在把约车时间改到明早五点。

早上？航班不是晚上吗？

What time should we leave for the airport?

I have a car service coming at 7.

But isn't our flight at 9:30?

Yes. Why?

Seven. Wow. Okay. So 7:00 is cutting it close, don't
    you think?

For a 9:30 flight?

Fine. Whatever. Do what you want.

Don't be like that. I'll do 6:45.

Sure.

Seriously? That's not early enough?

If it were me I would do 6:15. Maybe even 6:00. The
    405 is a nightmare.

But we've already checked in. And we have no bags
    to check.

Ahh, hello? Security lines?

Why are you talking like that?

Whatever.

I'm calling now. I'm making it for 6:00.

Five forty-five might be smarter.

You've got to be kidding me.

I don't kid about traffic.

Did you take something?

Look. All I'm saying is that if it were me, I'd do 5:30.
I would make it for 5:30.

Why not 5:00?

I don't know if that's your sarcastic voice but I agree
a hundred percent.

Okay then. I am now calling and making a
reservation for a car at 5:00 A.M. tomorrow.

A.M.? Isn't the flight in the evening?

我们说了彼此的……

知道吗？这是最烂的一家酒店，
你说。
你正在晚宴上
兴致勃勃地讲着
那个可怕的假期。
那些房间……
都是烟味，我插了句，
因为我觉得我表述得更好，
但你继续讲着，
嘘，戴维。烟臭味，我们就要求……
我们要求换房间！三次！我说，但是……
所有房间闻起来都一个味，戴维！
都是烟味，我盯着你，不必要地补充了一句。
现在是我在讲。
即便是你开始讲的，
但我想我们都同意一点——
我表述得更好。
但我感觉到你似乎不认同，
因为你盯着我，用不悦的口吻冷冷地说：

现在是我在讲。

接着你说：所以，我们问前台那个可爱的小个子……

不不不，在问之前，我们看到一个男的在抽烟……

我们问了前台之后才看到的……

不，之前。然后我们问前台，你们这里没有无烟房吗？

他回答……

哦，是的，您可以在所有房间里抽烟！

你有时候真的很浑蛋，你说。

之后，房间陷入了安静。

然后我说，酒店前台没对我们说浑蛋的话，只说了抽烟的事。

有段时间没人请我们参加晚宴了，

是吧？

We finish each other's . . .

You guys, it was the worst hotel ever

you said.

You were telling the story

at the dinner party

about the horrible vacation.

The rooms . . .

Smelled of cigarette smoke, I said, jumping in

because I think I tell it better.

But you kept going.

Shh, David. Cigarette smoke. And we asked . . .

We asked to switch rooms! Three times! I said. But ...

All the rooms smelled the same. David!

Like smoke, I added, needlessly,

looking at you, because I was telling it.

Even though you were telling it first.

But I think we can agree that seriously

I tell it better.

But I get the sense that you don't agree.

Because you looked at me and said in your quiet

angry voice,

I'm telling it.

And you said *So we ask this adorable little man at the
front desk . . .*

No no. Before that we see a guy smoking . . .

We saw him after we went to the front desk . . .

No. Before. And we ask the guy, Do you have any
non- smoking rooms.

And he says . . .

Oh yes, you can smoke in any of them!

You are such an asshole sometimes, you said.

It got quiet after that.

And then I said, the concierge didn't say the asshole
part to us, just the smoke thing.

We haven't been invited to a dinner party in a while
have we?

海鲜？

想告诉你，
在我从商场
开车回家的路上，
我听了碧昂丝那首美妙的歌曲。

我忘了歌名，
但歌词内容
我深以为然。

有一段
特别赞：
"如果他让本姑娘满足了，
本姑娘就带他去吃龙虾。"

很有意思，不是吗？
巧的是，值得期待的
龙虾大餐
正等你来拿。

若你选择加入
本次活动，
我很愿领你去
大啖龙虾。（哈哈哈！）

不要吗？
也好。
我们随便弄点儿吃的吧。

Seafood?

I meant to tell you
as I was driving home from
the mall earlier
I heard that marvelous song by Beyoncé.

I forget the name
but she sings
about things
that I liked a lot.

One in particular
was this.
When he fuck me good
I take his ass to Red Lobster.

Isn't that interesting?
And the funny thing is
Shrimp Fest
is going on right now.

I would be happy to take your behind (ha ha!)
to the restaurant of your choice
were you to uphold
your part of the deal.

No?
Very good.
We could also just do chicken.

亲密关系心理咨询（第二部分）

我承认，
我不该问 Wi-Fi。
我也承认，
我没有倾听和尊重艾米。
我还要承认，
我讨厌"承认"这个词。

"这就是我要说的。"
艾米对咨询师说，
咨询师随即让她
直接把感受告诉罗杰。
"好吧，罗杰，我听出了
你语气中的恼火，
你也根本就不承认你的'承认'。"
"我不承认。"我大声说，
真没想到，
我以为我只会在心里说这些。
"蠢货。"你说。

"艾米，"咨询师说，"他的名字是罗杰。"

"真的吗？"艾米问，

"因为在我看来，他就像个蠢货。"

Couples counseling (part 2)

I acknowledge that
I shouldn't have asked about Wi-Fi.
And I acknowledge that I wasn't
listening to or respecting Amy.
I would also like to acknowledge
that I hate the word "acknowledge."

This is what I'm talking about
Amy says to the therapist,
who then asks Amy to acknowledge her feelings
by speaking directly to Roger.
Fine. Roger, I'm hearing from the tone
of your voice
that you are exasperated and don't mean your
    acknowledgment.
I don't, I say
out loud
which is a surprise
as I thought I was only thinking it.

Dickhead, you say.

Amy, the therapist says. *His name is Roger.*

Really? Amy asks.

Because he looks to me like a dickhead.

你和朋友外出后，
你妈打来电话，我想对她说——

你女儿和朋友出去了，

我一个人和孩子们在一起，我说。

太好了，她说。

小宝贝们都好吗？

你好吗，史蒂夫？

我？很好，挺好的。

你的声音怎么有些奇怪啊？她说。

哦，你懂的，

生活、工作、压力，还有这些个孩子，

没什么，

但很多时候，我都被一种深深的悲伤

笼罩着。

我以为这很正常。

你是否有过奄奄一息的感觉？

看到一个岔路口，却怎么也想不起路名，

没有吗？哦。

什么？是的，我刚开了瓶酒，怎么了？

这就像公交车的车轮，

会不停地转啊转，

这很自然。

要不它们还能做什么？

还有这个该死的雨刮，

如果它一直这样刷来刷去、刷来刷去，

你就该把它给换掉。

老天啊！

我其实想对你说的是：

嗨，芙兰，你好吗？

What I meant to say to your mother when she called and you were out with friends

Your daughter is out with friends
and I am here alone with the kids, I said.
How nice, she said.
How are my grandkids?
How are you, Steve?
Me? I'm fine. Fine.
Your voice sounds a little strange, she said.
Oh, you know.
Life and work and stress and the kids.
It's fine.
But I do find a kind of deep sadness
overwhelms me mostdays.
I think that's pretty common though.
Do you ever feel like you're dying?
Ever look at a fork and have no idea of the name of it?
No? Oh.
What? Yes, that's a cork being opened, why?

I guess it's just that

of *course* the wheels
on the bus go round and round.
What else would they do?
And this fucking wipers situation.
If they go swish, swish, swish
you *have* to replace them.
I mean Jesus *Christ*!
What I meant to say was
Hey, Fran, how are you?

半夜里，你找我

你醒过来，
在黑暗中呻吟着。
一个可怕的梦？
或是头痛？
无论是哪一个，
你触碰着
我的身体。
我在这儿，我说着，
伸手去回应。
不过你仍在摸索着，
像掉了隐形眼镜，
而不像在找寻我的胯中物。
不过，这仍是段
难得的半夜小插曲，
要来点儿更狂放的吗？

当我开始抚摸你时，
你坐起身来，
完全醒了。

我要，你说。
我现在就给你，我说。

你干吗啊？你问，
我要找张面巾纸，
我鼻子太堵了。
好好睡你的觉去。

You reach for me in the middle of the night

You wake

moaning in the dark.

A dirty dream?

Or your head cold?

Either way

you reach for

my body.

Well hello there, I say,

reaching over for you.

Though you are still feeling around

like you've lost a contact lens

and not for my penis.

Still, a rare middle-of-the-night

interlude.

Care to be rude?

But as I caress you

you sit up

fully waking.

I need it, you say.

Then I'm your man, I say.

What are you doing? you ask.

I need a Kleenex.

My nose is running.

Go back to sleep.

来一起讨论下我的内衣

拉佩拉，

维秘，

CK。

如果你想要轻薄性感的内衣，

那你可以买这几个品牌，

然后自己穿上。

你为我折好了商品目录册里的页码，

"性感"，你批注道。

好贴心啊！

我是否问过你，

你的裤衩为啥穿得没有布拉德利·库珀性感？

没有吧，虽然我原本可以这样问。

你知道谁的产品线做得好？

沃尔玛，

那儿的内衣被称作"大裤衩"，

我喜欢这个名字。

白色的，一包五条，

上面写着：一个尺码适合所有人。

你可以把它们当降落伞，

或是吊床，

或是遮掩你那已过中年的臀部。

我喜欢把它们放在你面前，然后看着你的脸。

但……但……这些看起来像印度的兜迪，你说，

有些困惑。

我知道，我微笑着说，

而且都可以机洗，

这才是我对于性感的观点。

Let's talk about my underpants

La Perla.

Victoria's Secret.

Calvin Klein.

If you want skimpy, sexy lingerie

you should buy some.

And then wear them yourself.

You dog-ear the catalogues for me.

Hot, you write.

How sweet.

Do I ask you about your

Less-than-Bradley-Cooper-like boxers?

No. But I could.

Do you know who makes a great line?

Walmart.

It's called "Big Unders."

I like that name.

They're white, come five to a pack.

One size fits all, it says.

You could use them as a parachute.

Or a hammock.

Or to cover your middle-aged bum.

I like to put them on in front of you and watch your
    face.

But . . . but . . . those look like an Indian dhoti, you say,
    confused.

I know, I say, smiling.

And they're machine washable.

Now that's my idea of sexy.

不能正确组装宜家的橱柜，
我思索自己的男子气概

当我大声说道：

这个破玩意儿该装到哪儿？

我不是在问你，

我只是在说，这个破玩意儿该装到哪儿呢？

是的，此刻，我彻底意识到，

我装的和图纸示意的，大相径庭。

那是什么？你问。

嗯，我知道，也许我完全装反了。

该死。

不，不用打电话"找个人"问问，

我就是个"人"，

我能自己装好。

我不像你爸，能自个儿盖间小木屋。

也不像你前男友，"万能先生"，

懂土木建筑。

我也留不出

他那一脸大胡子。

我有张娃娃脸，

胡须也长得很随机。

而且，我不知道六角扳手和内六角扳手

在本质上功能相同。

我从没用过电锯，

也异常惧怕蟑螂，

但即便不是特种部队的候选人，

从严格的生物学观点上讲，

我还算是个男人。

没啥了不起的，我哭着说，

你来做吧！

While failing to correctly assemble an IKEA cabinet, I consider my manhood

When I say out loud
What the fuck is this piece for
I'm not asking you a question.
I'm saying what the fuck is this piece for.
And yes, I am fully aware that what I've made so far
does not look like the picture on the box.
What's that? you say.
Oh. I see. Maybe the whole thing is upside down.
Shit.
No, we're not going to call "a guy."
I'm a guy.
I can build things.
Not like your father, who built a cabin by himself.
Or your old boyfriend, mister wonderful
the contractor.
Nor can I grow a big beard
like him
because I have the face of a small boy

with random patches of kitten-like hair.

And no, I didn't know that a hex key and an Allen
wrench

were essentially the same thing.

And I have never used a power saw.

And am bizarrely afraid of water bugs.

But I am a man in the strictest biological sense

if not the ideal Special Forces candidate.

Big deal, I'm crying.

Here. You do it.

亲密关系心理咨询（第三部分）

让我们试一下
角色扮演吧，
咨询师说，
罗杰，
你先来。
还有，罗杰，
我们要记好：
角色扮演
不是你
在那儿假装
艾米，
现在是她的闺密
珍妮芙。

Couples counseling (part 3)

Let's try some

role play

the therapist says.

Roger

you start.

And Roger

let's remember that

role play

isn't where

you pretend

Amy

is her friend

Jennifer.

我们会有所不同

等以后
我们有了孩子，
他们基本上
不会看电视。

绘画和音乐，
将成为他们的
缪斯女神。

他们将从棋类
和纸牌游戏中
得到乐趣，
我们也是。

快进七年，
周日清晨六点，
爸爸和妈妈
昨夜聚会喝嗨了。

你知道谁是我们现在的缪斯女神？

答对了，

海绵宝宝，

一个接一个

再接一个新缪斯。

完全没问题，

你当然能用薄荷糖当早餐，

好孩子。

We will be different

When we have
children,
they will watch almost no
television.

Painting and drawing and music,
this will be their
muse.

Board games and cards.
What fun they will have.
Us too.

Fast forward
seven years
and it is 6 A.M.
on a Sunday morning
and Mommy and Daddy
had too much to drink at the party.

Do you know who our muse is now?

That's right

SpongeBob.

One after another

after another.

You're damn right

you can have Mentos

for breakfast, kids.

我问没孩子的同事蒂姆，
他周末过得怎么样

太——棒——了，他说，两眼放光，
非常棒的周末。
只有我和迈克。
我们睡了个懒觉，
去了间城里新开的店，
喝了杯咖啡。
你去过那儿吗？没有吗？
之后我们去中央公园散了会儿步，
逛了圈大都会博物馆的戈雅画展，
太震撼了。
你去看过吗？没有吗？
我们骑车去康尼岛，
在帝发拉餐厅吃比萨。
你吃过那家店吗？没有吗？
我以为你住在布鲁克林。
嗯。
去游了会儿泳，
找到家不错的冰激凌店，

坐火车回家后云雨一番，

完事后小睡片刻。

这不就是周末最好的时光吗？

性爱和小憩？

你的表情好奇怪。

然后我们一时兴起，

买了两张音乐剧《汉密尔顿》的黄牛票。

你看过吗？没有吗？真的吗？哇。

这是我们第三次看。

后来我们发现了一家惊艳的爵士酒吧，待到凌晨四点。

之后走到皇后区大桥，去看日出。

最后回家，一觉睡到晌午。

你周末过得怎么样？

嗯，蒂姆，我们去出奇老鼠连锁餐厅参加了

一个孩子的生日聚会，

和其他家长闲扯了几句，

也没什么共同话题。

你参加过吗？没有吗？会有惊喜哦。

I ask my coworker, Tim, who doesn't have children, how his weekend was

A-ma-zing, he says, eyes wide.

It was amazing.

Just me and Michael.

We slept in

got coffee at that new place

in the Village.

Have you been? No?

Then we strolled through Central Park.

Wandered over to the Goya show at the Met.

Incredible.

Have you seen it? No?

Rode Citi Bikes to Coney Island.

Had pizza at Di Fara's.

You've eaten there right? No?

I thought you lived in Brooklyn.

Huh.

Went for a swim.

Found a great ice cream place.

Took the train back to our place and had sex.

Took a nap.

Isn't that the best part of the weekend?

Sex and naps?

You have a weird expression.

Then on a whim we

bought scalper tickets for *Hamilton*.

Have you seen it? No? Really? Wow.

This was our third time.

Later we found this amazing jazz club and stayed till

    four.

We walked over the Fifty-Ninth Street Bridge and

    watched the sun come up.

Then we went home and slept till noon.

How was your weekend?

Well, Tim, we went to a kid's birthday party at

Chuck E. Cheese

And made inane small talk

with other parents we have nothing in common with.

Have you been? No? Amazing.

晚饭吃点儿什么

宛若燕子如期飞至卡皮斯特拉诺教堂，
每天下班前你都给我打电话，
说几句不痛不痒的口水话。
这和燕子的到访没啥关联，
我只是在想，那些燕子每年的迁徙，
都像上了发条一样，沿着同一条该死的路线。

嘿，还好吗？你心不在焉地问我，
同时看着邮件。
晚饭吃点儿什么？
不知道，我边回答
边在某个时尚网站上看着一款手袋。
我在工作呢，跟你一样。
吃点儿鸡肉？你问道。
我点开了 ESPN 网站上的《身体特刊》[1]。

行啊，我说，已然忘记我们在讨论什么。
你能买点儿冰激凌吗？你问道，
点开了《赫芬顿邮报》官网。

你是叫我订点儿外卖吗？我边说
边放大着瑞安·雷诺兹的照片。
我可以去，你说道，
用耗尽能量的声线，好像你刚收到一则死讯。

我们有些剩的意大利面，我边说
边想象着瑞安·雷诺兹在四季酒店的裸照。
我讨厌吃剩饭，你说，就像上了发条一样，老套乏味。
我打赌瑞安·雷诺兹一点儿也不老套乏味，
没想到我大声说出了最后一句。

1　《身体特刊》会邀请知名男女运动员拍摄裸体写真，展现运动与人
　体之美。(本书注释如无特别说明，均为译者注。)

What's the plan for dinner?

Like swallows to Capistrano
you call me each afternoon from work.
Quick point on the swallows thing.
I'm not saying swallows call.
I guess I just mean they perform, on schedule,
the same damned ritual.

Hey. What's up? you say, distracted,
reading an email.
What's the plan for dinner?
I don't know, I say
looking at a purse on the Fossil site.
I'm at work. Like you.
Chicken? you ask
toggling over to the Body Issue of espn.com.

Sure, I say, already having forgotten what we're
  talking about.

Can you get ice cream? you ask
clicking over to huffpo.
So I'm getting dinner then, I say
enhancing a picture of Ryan Reynolds.
I can get it, you say, drained of energy
as if you've just received news of a death.

We have leftover pasta, I say
picturing Ryan Reynolds naked in a Four Seasons
      hotel room.
I hate leftovers, you say, swallow-like, so predictable.
I bet Ryan Reynolds isn't predictable.
Except I say that last part out loud.

我们的爱情在路上受到了考验

当上帝
堵在环城高速上
以时速六公里向前爬行时，他会如何行动？
我来告诉你他可能不会做哪些事。
他不会冲着一辆
无意插到我们前面的
贴有残障人士标志的福特福克斯里的
老太太大喊：
臭婊子。
因为这很不好，而且也可能并非实情。

我现在到底怎么不支持你了？
好吧，我们再也不要去海滩了。
很对，我们应该早点儿离开。
是的，孩子们今天会睡得很晚，这会毁了你的生活。
我知道，我们到家的时候，卖酒的商店已经打烊了。

哇，你这满嘴问候谁谁父母的话，
拜托考虑下后排座位上的孩子们，好吗？

也许现在问这个有点儿不合时宜，
不过你怒赞过的那款
禅修应用，
有效果吗？

Our love is tested in traffic

What would Jesus do
in this bumper-to-bumper mess on the BQE
going four miles an hour?
I'll tell you what he probably wouldn't do.
He wouldn't call the old woman in the Ford Focus
with the handicapped plates
who slipped in ahead of us
a cocksucker.
Because that's not nice. And probably not true.

How exactly am I not supporting you right now?
Fine, we'll never go to the beach again.
Okay, we should have left earlier.
Yes, the kids will get to bed late and that ruins your
        life.
I know, the wine store will be closed by the time we
        get home.

Wow, that was a string of astounding obscenities.

You know the kids are in the back seat, right?

Is now the wrong time to ask
how that Buddhist meditation app
you raved about
is working out for you?

我可否不再参加孩子学校的志愿服务

早先，

在学校的嘉年华上，

一位不知姓名的家长说：

你妻子说你要负责充气屋！

那是最糟糕的事，哈哈哈！

我不知道我会负责充气屋，

也不知道那是最糟糕的。

我一直以为棉花糖机

才是最麻烦的。

那是去年

你让我去负责的。

那天 32 度，潮湿，没有遮阴处，

其他的父母在挥手和微笑，

也许他们是在笑话我？

我认为是的。

我严重脱水，

身上挂满了糖丝。

孩子们在哭闹。

这看上去不像棉花糖，
一位生气的母亲说道。
我想回句，"去死吧"，
但我忍住了，
或许我的表情已说明了一切？

现在
已过晌午。
看不到冰镇啤酒，
我那汗淋淋、湿漉漉、强颜欢笑的脸，
卡在一块画着谷仓背景的
胶合板中，
我成了一头戴着高筒大礼帽的
肥猪。
孩子们在开怀大笑，
他们把派扔到我脸上，
真的很疼。
"哈哈哈！你看保罗。"
你笑着说，
你的脸很干净，上面也没有派，
"他喜欢当志愿者。"
不，他不喜欢。
保罗讨厌这种烂工作。

Would it be possible to stop volunteering me for things?

Earlier

at the school carnival

a parent whose name I don't know said

Your wife said you were doing the bounce house!

That's the worst ha ha!

I didn't know that I was doing the bounce house.

Or that it was the worst.

I assumed the cotton candy machine

was the worst.

That's what you volunteered me for

last year.

It was ninety degrees and humid and no shade.

Other parents waving and smiling.

Or were they laughing at me?

I think they were.

But I was badly dehydrated

covered with spun sugar.

Kids crying.

That doesn't look like cotton candy
one angry mother said.
Go die, I wanted to say
But didn't.
Though maybe my expression did?

And now
late in the afternoon
Not a cold beer in sight
my sweaty, sticky forced-smile face
wedged through
a hole in a piece of plywood
painted to look like a barnyard.
And I am a fat pig
wearing a stovepipe hat.
The kids are laughing now
because they are throwing pies in my face.
And it kind of hurts.
Ha ha! Look at Paul
you say, laughing.
Your face clean and pie free
He loves to volunteer.
No, he doesn't.
Paul hates this shit.

亲密关系心理咨询（第四部分）

咨询师给我们留了些作业。
列张清单，她说，
写下你们喜欢对方的什么。
你咝溜咝溜地喝汤，
那咂嘴的声音
在不停地折磨我。
你说在中国，饭后打个饱嗝
是对厨师表达敬意的方式。
这简直是瞎扯，
再说现在我们人在芝加哥。
"我现在是老牛拉犁——有心无力啊！"
你笑着说。
也许吧，
但我完全可以宰掉那头牛。

这写的是什么？你问。
哦，没什么，亲爱的，
你的清单列得怎么样了？

Couples counseling (part 4)

The therapist gave us homework.
Make a list, she said.
Of the things you love
about each other.
You slurp soup.
That sucking sound
is killing me.
You say that burping after a meal in China is a
show of respect for the cook.
I think that's bullshit.
Also we live in Chicago.
You can't teach an old dog new tricks
you say, laughing.
Perhaps.
But you can put an old dog down and kill it.

What's that? you ask.
Oh nothing, honey.
How's your list?

写给你那位精神类药理学家的赞歌

亲爱的，以毫克为单位

分发爱情的药剂师，

炼金术士，

配制高手，

调酒达人。

丈夫：很听话。

婚姻：被挽救。

如果我们没找到

舍曲林和立普能[1]之间的

完美搭配，

我将不会在我丈夫身边。

医术高明，

感激涕零。

---

1 舍曲林、立普能：均为抗抑郁药。

Ode to your psychopharmacologist

Dear doctor pill man

who doles out love in milligrams.

Alchemist.

Magic mix.

Mixologist.

Husband: behaved.

Marriage: saved.

I would not be around

had we not found

that perfect combo

of Zoloft and Lexapro.

You're a pro.

I thank you so.

深思熟虑后，
我后悔我们没能早点儿离开公司的假日派对

我们和我的老板同乘电梯，

我刚得到这份喜欢的新工作。

你，我的丈夫，喝多了。

他，没喝那么多。

你背对着电梯门，

离他那么近，

他看上去不太舒服，

我感到难堪。

很可爱的派对，他对你说着，

一边往后退，试图缩进电梯墙壁里。

你看上去才可爱呢，你毫无逻辑地说，

然后你抱住他

并把头靠到他肩上。

他说，哦，天哪。

而你轻声唱起：

当一个男人爱上一个女人。

就是这样。

Upon reflection, I wish we had left my company holiday party a little earlier

We rode the elevator down with my boss.
My new boss at the new job I really like.
You, my husband, drunk.

      Him, not so much.
You stood so close to him
your back to the elevator door.
He looked uncomfortable.
I cringed.

    Lovely party, he said to you

        trying to pull himself back into the elevator wall.

    You're a lovely party, you said.

        Which made no sense.
Then you hugged him
and put your head on his shoulder.

    And he said, *Oh my*

        while you sang, softly sang,

           When a man loves a woman.

So there's that.

（俳句是由十七个音节组成的日本短诗，分为音节是五、七、五的三行，传统上多是对自然景象的描绘和感受。）

为何是俳句
因我的离婚律师
查出你偷腥

……

快拨"911"
你裤裆拉链上方
卡着半只鸟

……

"她胸好大啊"
你放肆地评论着
我无地自容

……

致我新公婆
不打招呼就到家
断然拒开门

(*Editor's note: a haiku is a Japanese poem of seventeen syllables, in three lines of five, seven, and five, traditionally evoking images of the natural world.*)

Why a haiku Stu?
Because my divorce lawyer
Found your girlfriend's text

. . .

I'll call nine-one-one
Because your penis is stuck
In your zipper hon

. . .

Pam's got quite a rack
Is not what I want to hear
When you meet my friends

. . .

To my new in-laws
You keep stopping by, no call
I won't open door.

母亲节

我不知道近藤麻理惠是谁。

国际畅销书

《怦然心动的人生整理魔法》的作者。

这是多么有趣的母亲节礼物啊。

我们应该如何用"爱"来叠衣服,

我们应该如何只保留"怦然心动"的东西。

不会让我怦然心动很多次的,

你知道是什么吗?

你。

我应该保留你吗?

这张卡片很贴心,

"你知道你是什么吗?"

怪诞的封面上写着这么一个问题。

"一个妈妈!"

然后,是你的签名:

"你的丈夫,拉塞尔。"

这肯定让我的心活动了一会儿。

Mother's Day

I didn't know who Marie Kondo was.
Author of the international best-seller
The *Life-Changing Magic of Tidying Up*.
What a funny, funny
Mother's Day gift that was.
How we should fold clothes with "love."
How we should only keep things that "spark joy."
You know what doesn't spark joy
for me a lot of times?
You.
Should I keep you?
And the card was a thoughtful touch.
"You know what you are?"
It asked on the wacky cover.
"A mother!"
And you signed it
Your husband, Russell.
That certainly sparked something for me.

我在诉说前列腺检查的不适，
你的表情却告诉我……

宝贝，

你无法想象，

那有多不舒服，

当一根男人的手指

插入你的肛门。

而你的表情显示你丝毫不为所动。

你无法想象那种疼痛，

好比猛灌一口烈酒，

我是指，当他压着我前列腺的时候。

你点点头，

双臂环抱。

那我该怎么想象呢？你问道。

自然分娩？

不用药物？

不打无痛分娩针，

生出个八斤半的宝宝？

你再说下那位医生的手指有多粗？

Thoughts on the expression on your face while I explain the discomfort of my recent prostate exam

Honey
you have no idea
how uncomfortable it is
having a man's finger up your ass.
Though your face suggests
that you are unimpressed.

You have no idea what pain like that feels like,
I say, pouring a large gin.
I mean, he's pressing against my prostate.

You nod.
Arms folded.
How could I? you ask.
Natural childbirth.
No drugs.
No epidural.
Nine pounds five ounces.
How big was the doctor's finger again?

你对我的一丝惦念

谢谢你，
对我生日的
一丝惦念。
你问我想要什么，
我说什么都不要，
但你又问了一次。
我说：也许首饰吧，
耳环挺好。
比如钻石的，
你神秘地笑着说，
我也笑了。
然后是我的生日，
你送我一张
香蕉共和国的礼品卡。
我记得它们那儿有首饰，
你说。
那儿确实有首饰，但
不是钻石的。
谢谢。

You sort of thought of me

Thank you for thinking of me
sort of
on my birthday.
You asked me what I wanted
and I said oh nothing.
But you asked again
and I said jewelry might be nice.
Earrings maybe.
Diamond ones
you said with a sly smile.
And I smiled too.
And then it was my birthday
and you gave me a gift card to
Banana Republic.
I think they have jewelry there
you said.
They sure do. But
not diamonds.
Thank you.

我的结扎手术

没错，我们有四个孩子，
而且我在老三出生后，
保证过不会再生更多。

我就想说，我不明白，
你为啥非要
亲自来手术室。

还有，亲爱的，
医生是不会让你
亲手给我做结扎的。

等等，
他会的。
亲爱的，亲爱的……

你笑了起来，说，
可四十岁怀第四个孩子，
也不是件好事。

你脸上的表情有点儿怪啊,

亲爱的?

小心点。

My vasectomy

yes, we have four children
and I promised we wouldn't have more
after the third

that said, i don't know why
you have to be here
in person, in the surgical room

and no, honey, the doctor
is not going to let you make
the snip

oh wait
he is
honey honey honey

to which you laugh
and say

it wasn't a good idea to

get pregnant at forty with our fourth child, either.

you have a weird look on your face,

honey?

careful.

150

致丽莎，

非玩笑话

你打电话约我，
说你和朋友要去间酒吧喝啤酒、玩滚球。

我有些惊讶，
那时我们还不很熟络，
但深秋周日的夜晚，
我们喝着啤酒，
如老友般畅谈。

你的朋友从未出现，
他们曾到过吗？
天色已晚，我们离开酒吧
站在街角，
四周飘荡着几丝喝酒聊天之外的气息。

如果那天晚上我不愿离开公寓——
毕竟待在家里更简单些，
独自一人更容易些，
但你摧毁了我那惆怅的小生活，
你吻了我。

事情就这样奇妙地发生了，
若我们刚才在街角分开，
我的一生都会如同虚度。

我在巴黎的一座
老教堂旁的喷泉对面的
咖啡馆里，
向你求婚。

我想，我当时只想说：
感谢你，
感谢你拯救了我的生活，
感谢你让我不再是那个从前的我，
感谢你在离开会更容易时，选择了等候。

感谢露露和休伊特。

我们碰到过一个家伙，
他坐在长椅上吹奏着卡祖笛，
穿得像个小丑，
还戴着副滑雪镜，
那可是在夏天。

"你本来会变成那副模样，"你笑着说，
"如果你没遇到我的话。"
这很可能是真的。
我相信你已经做得很好，
不可能更好了。

我只希望即便没有诗歌，
你也能了解这些。

154

To Lissa.
No kidding.

You called me
and said you were meeting friends
for beers at a bar that had bocce.

I was surprised.
We knew each other
though not well.
But Sunday evening
in late fall we drank beer
and talked like old friends.

Your friends never showed.
Were they ever coming?
It got late and we left.
Standing on the corner,

it didn't feel like just meeting for a beer anymore.

I hadn't wanted to leave my apartment that evening.
Because it was easier to stay in.
It was easier to be alone.

Except you ruined my sad little life.
You kissed me.

How strange that it happens like that.
If we had just parted at the corner.
A whole life never lived.

I proposed in Paris
at a café across from a fountain
by an old church.

I guess I just wanted to say
thank you.

For saving my life.

For helping me un-become the person I was.

For staying when it would have been easier to
leave.

For Lulu and Hewitt.

We passed a guy on a bench once.

He was playing a kazoo

partially dressed like a clown

and wore ski goggles.

It was summer.

That would have been you, you said, smiling.
If you hadn't met me.

And it's probably true.

It's certainly true that you

could have done better.

But I most assuredly could not.

I just hope it doesn't take a poet
for you to know that.

致谢

出版这本诗集并非我的主意，如果你不喜欢的话，请去指责伊万·霍尔德。伊万是普特南出版社的董事长，也是个亲切和善的人。他和我的编辑兼挚友萨利·基姆给了我出版此书的建议。一开始我很犹豫，但之后他们说会给我些钱，我当即就答应了下来。因此，我要感谢他们。

同时，还要由衷地感谢《纽约客》的苏珊·莫里森。苏珊几年前很友善地在杂志上发表了我写的组诗《献给已婚人士的情人节诗歌》。据我所知，这是《纽约客》历史上阅读量最大、最受喜爱、被分享和谈论得最多的作品（尽管我没有证据，而且有可能记错了）。

我还要感谢普特南出版社和企鹅出版社的善人们，他们为这些诗提供了很多好建议，在此就不一一列举了。

我要感谢几位素未谋面的人，真正的诗人：玛丽·豪威、玛丽·奥利弗、约翰·奥多诺休、大卫·怀特、谢莫斯·希尼和比利·柯林斯。（对于他们的成就，我就不妄自评价了，感兴趣的朋友可以搜索"诗歌基金会"，它有个非常棒的网站，里面有丰富的诗歌和关于诗人的文章。）

感谢以下乐于阅读和评论本书初稿的朋友：露易丝·多尔蒂、贝基和布莱恩·格雷、黛比·凯瑟、利亚·马斯特罗贝蒂、蒂姆·勒加洛、迈克尔·比蒂、迪伦·米兹纳、妮可·桑兹，以及我的兄弟蒂姆·肯尼，他的评论是"我还以为这些诗会很搞笑呢"，这是非常有帮助的编辑建议。

衷心地感谢我的岳母兼好友琳达·芬克，她的审稿和编辑工作，让这本书变得更好。

还有我的妻子丽莎。我在《纽约客》上发表了那些诗后，一位邻居拦住了她，说："我很遗憾看到了约翰写的那些关于你的诗，还有你那条宽松的内裤。"作品写的不是她或我们的事，都是虚构的。我非常幸运，能够与这样一位女性结婚——她是我最好的朋友，几乎每天我都会给她发短信，告诉她："我已经迫不及待和你共度良宵了。"

丽莎，如果你正在阅读此文，那我要告诉你：我真的很喜欢你，如果你有兴趣的话，我们就尽快把今晚的时间空出来安排一下。如果你没有，我也完全理解。

ACKNOWLEDGMENTS

This book was not my idea. If you haven't enjoyed it, please blame Ivan Held. Ivan is president of G. P. Putnam's Sons and a lovely man. He and my editor and dear friend Sally Kim suggested it. I was hesitant at first, but then they said they would give me money and I immediately saw what a good idea it was. So I would like to thank them.

Also, a large thanks to Susan Morrison of *The New Yorker*. Susan was kind enough to publish a piece I wrote a few years ago, "Valentine's Day Poems for Married People," which I am told is the most read, most loved, most emailed, and most talked-about piece in the history of *The New Yorker* magazine (although I have no proof of that and I may be thinking of something else).

I would also like to thank the good people at Putnam and Penguin who provided ideas for poems, too many to list here.

I would like to thank a few people I do not know. Real poets. Marie Howe, Mary Oliver, John O'Donoghue, David

Whyte, Seamus Heaney, and Billy Collins. (I can't recommend their work enough. Check out the Poetry Foundation. It's a wonderful site and a deep well of poems and writing about poets.)

My thanks to friends who were kind enough to read and comment on early drafts. Louise Dougherty, Becky and Brian Gray, Debbie Kasher, Lea Mastroberti, Tim LeGallo, Michael Beatty, Dylan Mizner, Nicole Sands, and my brother, Tim Kenney, whose comment, "I thought these were supposed to be funny," was helpful editorial direction.

A huge thanks to my mother-in-law and pal, Linda Funke, for reading, editing, and making all of this better.

And my wife, Lissa. When I wrote the piece in *The New Yorker*, a neighbor of ours stopped my wife and said, "I'm so sorry John wrote all those poems about you. And also about your baggy underpants." The piece wasn't about her or us. They were made up. I count myself exceptionally lucky to be married to a woman who is my best friend and who I text most days to say, *I can't wait for our evening.*

Lissa, if you are reading this, I am fond of you and we should make out soon, if that is something that would be of interest to you. If not, I totally understand.